Apr.10/96
NOV 16 '95

Children in History

Acknowledgements

Our thanks are due to the Parkway Group for the design and lay-out of this edition. The illustrations on pages 26 and 28 are based on the drawings from *Houses* by Margaret and Alexander Potter, published by John Murray.

Children in History

The Middle Ages

Molly Harrison

Illustrations by Sheila Maguire

Hulton Educational Publications

© Molly Harrison
1959
ISBN 0 7175 0754 8

First published this format 1976 by Hulton Educational Publications Ltd.,
Raans Road, Amersham, Bucks.

Printed in Great Britain at the
University Printing House, Cambridge
(Euan Phillips, University Printer)

Contents

1 Read this first

THE Middle Ages lasted a very long time—from about the arrival of the Normans in 1066, until about the end of the Wars of the Roses, in 1485. They did not, of course, begin in a certain year and end in another year. People and customs and the things people make do not usually change suddenly, but alter gradually from one person's lifetime to that of their children and grandchildren.

Of course people living then did not think of their time as "The Middle Ages"—they just thought of it as "now". Calling this period "The Middle Ages" is only a convenient label for people since then who have written history books and for those who learn about history. When history came to be written down, after the invention of printing in the 15th century, the only records available were those of very early times. To the new historians the gap between those early times and their own seemed to be "the middle". But in fact there is no real middle, and no beginning and no end either, to the long story of people and the things they have made and used and the deeds they have done.

This is not merely a story about children only, for boys and girls have never at any time lived apart from their parents if they could help it. This is the first part of a story which has boys and girls at its centre. It is a true story and perhaps when you read it you may feel a little of what it was like to be 10 or 12 years old in England hundreds of years ago.

The story is true, but I hope you will not just believe that without thinking. I hope you will wonder, now and again as you read, how I know about these people living so long ago. How *do* we know about history? For naturally nobody living now could possibly have actually seen those people.

Probably your first thought may be that somebody told somebody who told somebody else, and so on. That is, of course, the way in which a lot of news and information does get about, but we know that it is not a reliable way. I should not expect you to believe that any history books were true if the writers had to depend merely upon hearsay and gossip for what they wrote.

Your next idea may be that we know "from books". But what books? There were no printed books at all in the Middle Ages, for William Caxton did not put up his printing press, the first in England, until 1480. Before printing was invented there were books, written by hand on a kind of skin called parchment. They were called manuscripts, from two Latin words which mean "written by hand". This was a long and tedious job and the monks who wrote the books must have enjoyed painting the beautiful little coloured pictures which they put in the margins of their pages, and here and there among the lettering.

Usually there were people in these pictures and, of course, they were copied from the people the monks saw around them, in towns and villages. If we look carefully at these drawings we can see the kind of clothes that the real men and women, boys and girls, of those days wore, and some of the things they used and made. You may find that there is one of these manuscripts in your local museum or in a nearby cathedral or church. If so, it is well worth while asking if you may see it, but of course you will not be allowed to handle it, for it would be very fragile and very precious.

Costume worn by the richer people

In old churches, too, there are often other clues to tell us about medieval people. You can often see stone statues or wooden carvings of figures, "brasses" with drawings of people engraved on them, and stained glass windows with figures of everyday people alongside angels and saints. Most of these show us grown-up people, but as we shall see, children dressed very like their parents.

Perhaps you have heard of the Bayeux tapestry. This is a very long and narrow piece of embroidery which was worked, probably by Norman ladies who had settled in England, soon after the invasion of this country by William of Normandy and his army. It can still be seen in Bayeux, in the North of France, and there are copies in the Victoria and Albert Museum, in London, and in the museum at Reading. The tapestry was worked to celebrate the Conquest and shows us mostly soldiers, busy with all sorts of jobs. But there are civilians too.

Most people could not read in those early days, but those who could, wrote letters to their friends and relations and a few of those letters can still be read. You and I could not read them, for the spelling is very different from ours, but scholars have worked out what they say and in reading them we can catch a glimpse of the thoughts and feelings and worries of people who were only interested in their "today" or "tomorrow" or "next month", and not in us, living six or seven hundred years afterwards.

Some people have always enjoyed writing down what they have done or seen, and the names of those whom they have met. Old diaries are precious clues to history but there are not many medieval ones left. Reports and government regulations there are, and Church and Court records, and these give us a glimpse, here and there, of what people were supposed to do and how, very often, they managed to do just what they wanted, in spite of the regulations.

A house being burned down by the Normans while a woman with her child escapes (Part of the Bayeux tapestry)

One of the greatest English poets lived and wrote during the Middle Ages. He was Geoffrey Chaucer and is best known for *The Canterbury Tales* which is a fine collection of stories about typical medieval people. From these stories we know a great deal about the details of daily life in the fourteenth century, when Chaucer lived, and the kind of things that made people happy, or angry, or sad.

In the early Middle Ages most people did not have surnames, as we all have now. They were known by their baptismal or "Christian" names, and often the name of their father was added on. To avoid muddle it was the custom to add either the name of the place where a person lived, or his trade, or something which described him. Many of the most usual names of today were popular then: Mary, Margaret, Anne, Peter, Paul, John, Robert, Stephen, Richard. Added to these were descriptions like the Short, Longshanks, Brown, Bull, Baker or Litelmus (little mouse) or less obvious names like Stepsoft, Barefoot, Pluckenhenn, Mabel Yokedogge, Alice Writhecol (who was evidently always twisting her neck about), Swetemilke, Sourmilk and Gotobed!

You may like to look up other medieval names and choose one for yourself before you start to read this true story. . . .

Things to do and talk about

1 Start a scrap-book about boys and girls in the Middle Ages and add drawings, paintings and newspaper cuttings as you go along.

2 Make a 'Then and Now' book with pictures of medieval objects on one side and corresponding things of today on the other.

3 Look at this list of fifty surnames which owe their origin to trades, crafts and professions. Try to find out what jobs were done by craftsmen with these names. Some of the names are obvious but some of them are more obscure. What other names can you find?

On each of the *things to do* pages which follow in this book you will see a figure of one of the famous pilgrims mounted on a horse. See if you can find out the name of each pilgrim from this list (not in the same order). The Monk, The Squire, The Prioress, The Merchant, The Miller, The Cook, The Clerk of Oxford, The Wife of Bath, Chaucer.

Cloth Industry	Merchants and Shopkeepers			Other Crafts, etc.
Walker	Sherman	Merchant	Tanner	Warner
Fuller	Brewer	Chandler	Barker	Miller
Tucker	Brewster	Draper	Skinner	Wheeler
Dyer	Butcher	**Builders**	**Metal Workers**	Milner
Lister	Baker	Mason	Smith	Butler
Weaver	Baxter	Carpenter	Wright	Barber
Webster	Chapman	Tiler	**Farming**	Potter
Webber	Spicer	Slater	Farmer	Leech
Webb	Cook	Thatcher	Shepherd	Clark
Spinner	Mercer	Paynter	Coward	
Taylor		**Leather Workers**	Shearer	
		Sadler	Parker	

2 How they dressed

IF you had lived in England in the Middle Ages you would not have had nearly as many clothes as you have today. Whether your family was rich or poor, all the clothes had to be made at home. The thread had to be spun at home and the cloth woven there as well. All this took a long time, especially as so many other jobs had to be done at home too. Fortunately, however, these clothes were strong and did not wear out easily.

Babies were "swaddled" in linen. That is, they were rolled up tightly in linen cloth, because people believed that that would make their arms and legs grow straight. The cloth was then criss-crossed with coloured bands, until the baby looked very much like a mummy or a cocoon. He could not move anything but his head.

Babies are not swaddled nowadays, of course, and modern doctors and mothers would consider it very unhealthy. It was a very old custom, for you remember that Jesus had been "wrapped in swaddling clothes" when He was laid in the manger. That was about twelve hundred years before the Middle Ages, but babies were still dressed in much the same way.

On top of his swaddling bands a medieval baby would be wrapped in as many woollen shawls and blankets as his parents could afford. Houses were cold and draughty, so he needed plenty of extra covering for warmth. There was no shortage of wool in England, for this had for a very long time been a country where a lot of sheep were reared.

It was the custom for godmothers and godfathers to give a "christening shirt" as a present when a baby was baptised. These had little bands and cuffs embroidered in coloured thread. After the Middle Ages it became usual to give a special mug, spoon or plate as a christening gift instead of a shirt, and this is still the custom nowadays.

When he could sit up, the baby was put into a little frock,

Babies in swaddling bands

Tabard   Tunic and hood

Lady at her toilet

Later in the period

reaching down to his feet and tied in at the waist. It must have been very awkward for him when he was crawling!

Little boys and girls were dressed just alike. Underneath they probably wore a chemise and some kind of knickers. Over these they wore a short under-tunic, covered by a gown that reached down to their ankles. The gown was called a "cotte"—pronounced like our word "cot".

When he was six years old a boy no longer wore cottes, but was dressed very much like his father. He wore close-fitting, tight trousers, with feet. These were called "hose" and were tied to a short chemise by leather straps called "points". Over the hose he wore a tunic, or "tabard". The tabard had a belt and from this the boy would hang his pocket. Pockets were not part of the garment, as they are now. They were little bags, usually of leather, and you can see one hanging from the waist of the boy (page 18). In his pocket a boy kept his knife and any small treasures he possessed. If you turn out your own pockets you will notice how many of the things you keep in them a medieval boy or girl could not have had.

In cold weather a boy wore a surcoat over his tabard. This was rather like a long gym tunic, with very large armholes, and only sewn halfway up the sides. Over the surcoat he wore a pointed hood, with enough stuff in it round the neck to cover his shoulders.

Boys had their hair cut in a curious way. It was shaved halfway up the head at the back and cut straight across the forehead in front. From the front it looked very much as if a basin had been put on the boy's head and all the hair that showed round the edge of the basin cut off.

Until he was seven years old a boy from a well-off home lived with his father and mother, but when he reached that age he had to leave home, just as many boys and girls go away nowadays to boarding school. The medieval boy did not leave to go to school, however; he went to become a page in the household of a nobleman, where he would learn how to become a squire and, later, a knight. We shall see what he had to learn, later on.

After he left home the boy did not wear his own clothes any longer, but was dressed in the "livery", or uniform, of his master. It might be a tabard embroidered with his master's coat of arms, or he might have to wear hose, tabard and surcoat of a special colour, which could be easily recognised. Poor boys mostly stayed at home and helped their fathers in their work and continued to wear the same kind of clothes.

Girls were not so fortunate in their clothing as boys. They were kept all their lives in long gowns like their mothers', reaching down to the ground. Over these they wore a kind of surcoat and underneath they wore long petticoats, so that it must have been very difficult for them to run about when they wanted to. Perhaps such dresses were worn only on special occasions and a plain smock or overall for every day, but this, too, would have been very long.

Boys' hairstyles

On the whole there was little difference in shape between the clothes of children from rich families and those from poor ones. The cloth was different in quality, of course, but all the garments were very simple in shape, though wealthy children may sometimes have had theirs embroidered.

Poor children ran about barefoot, or bound their feet with strips of leather over warm straw padding. Rich ones wore soft shoes, without heels, made of cloth or leather. You wore leather gloves, too, if your family was well-off. As these had no gussets, they had to have slits down the back, so that you could bend your hands easily. Look and see if you can find on a modern glove where the slits used to be.

Shoes seem to have been very cheap, for in the 13th century a pair for a boy living in Oxford cost only two-pence halfpenny (about 1 p)! But a penny then was worth very much more in those days than it is now.

Wool, for making woollen cloth, was always spun at home. Boys and girls in the Middle Ages must have been very used to seeing their mothers and the servants busy spinning. You would often have heard the looms working in your home, too, and the thud-thud-thud as the batten beat the weft threads into the warp. The picture on page 23 shows you what warp and weft threads are.

Much linen cloth was imported into England from abroad. It was taken in exchange for English woollen cloth, which foreigners were glad to have. There was a rougher kind of linen, worn by poorer people, which was made at home in England.

Accessories: hat, shoes, purses and gloves, including peasant's working glove

Boy and girl wearing sleeveless surcoats.
These were sometimes fur-lined

The cheapest homespun cloth was made of undyed wool of the colour that was called hodden-grey. (Hodden meant "kept" and hodden-grey cloth was wool that was still of its natural greyish colour.) Workmen and most country people wore their clothes made of cloth of this dull colour, and probably children were generally dressed in it too. Country women sometimes dyed their stuffs with dyes made from roots and flowers, but the colours were rather soft ones. Fashionable ladies and gentlemen had their homespun dyed to all sorts of brilliant colours. These stuffs were usually sent abroad to be dyed and this was very expensive. So we can be sure that a medieval child seldom got anything more colourful than a gay cap or a bright belt, when his mother or older sister had a new gown.

WARP
THREADS

WEFT
THREADS

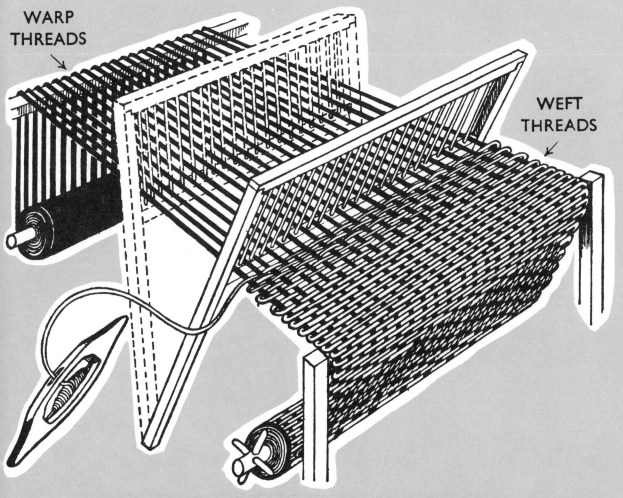

Diagram showing warp and weft threads

People were not allowed to wear what they liked in the Middle Ages, and there were many laws passed about what clothing might be worn. In the 14th century, for instance, there were complaints in Parliament that many people were dressing too extravagantly and an Act was passed to try to stop this. Here are some of the rules laid down:

Grooms and servants must not wear any cloth in their tunics or hose costing more than a certain sum of money, nor must they wear anything made of gold or silver on their garments. Their wives and children had to wear the same sort as the men. Wives and children of tradesmen were to wear "no veils, but such as are made with thread, nor any kind of furs, excepting those of lambs, rabbits, cats or foxes".

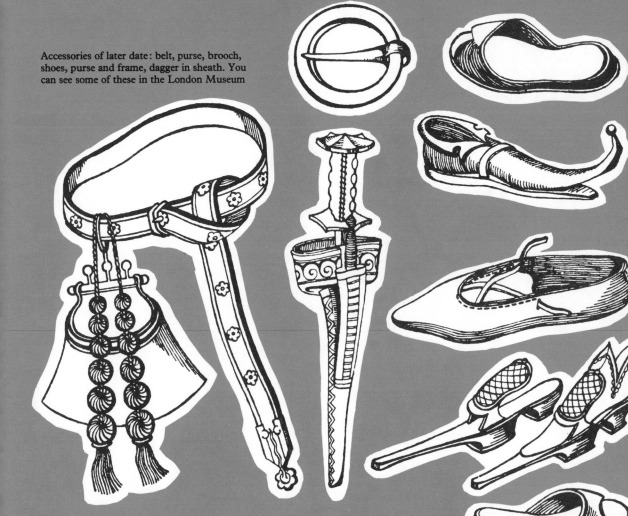

Accessories of later date: belt, purse, brooch, shoes, purse and frame, dagger in sheath. You can see some of these in the London Museum

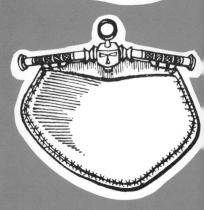

The wives and children of knights were not to wear linings of ermine fur in their garments. Ermine was considered to be a fur suitable only for kings, queens and nobles.

And it was said that "all labourers and lower classes of people shall wear no kind of cloth but blankets and russets (these were two kinds of very rough cloth), nor use any girdles than such as are made of linen". Grander people wore leather girdles.

The punishments for disobeying these rules were to have the garments taken away from you, but even so, it seems that people often managed to wear more or less what they liked, for new rules were constantly being made.

Things to do and talk about

1 Look for pictures of medieval people in churches: on tombstones, on memorial brasses, on stained glass windows, in wall paintings and perhaps in old records.

2 Look in museums for tapestries and embroideries showing how they dressed, and perhaps you may find a few pieces of real fabric—a sleeve, a glove or a collar. Why are there no complete medieval costumes to be seen anywhere?

3 Draw two outline figures and make sets of paper clothing to dress them in.

4 Look carefully at pictures of medieval people and see if you can dress up to look like one. You will not need a whole outfit—a hood, a nightdress, a pair of coloured tights, a vest, a minidress, a few pieces of cloth would all be useful. You could hold a medieval dress-parade with some friends.

Notice particularly the variety of head dress styles worn by the ladies in this picture.

3 Where they lived

THE kind of home you lived in in the Middle Ages depended, entirely, as it does now, upon whether your family was rich or poor. But it also depended upon which part of the country you lived in.

Nowadays if you travel about England you can see houses in one district very like those in another. This is because it is easy, with railways and good roads, to carry timber and stone and bricks and cement from one area to another.

But in earlier times people generally built with the materials they could most easily get. The roads were very bad in England and there were few bridges across the rivers. So it was almost impossible to carry heavy materials from place to place, though you might occasionally have seen a procession of pack-horses laden with building materials when some new church or grand house was being built.

In districts where there was a lot of good stone, houses were built of stone. This material varies in colour in different districts, so that you might have lived in a grey stone house, or a reddish or yellowish one according to which district of England your home was in.

If yours had been a rich family early in the Middle Ages, your home would have been a stone tower surrounded by a stone wall and moat. This was necessary for safety. Gradually, as life became safer, warlike castles were no longer necessary and many nobles had manor houses built. At first these had strong walls and tiny narrow windows like those of the castles, and their floors were of trodden earth, but these early manor houses were probably much more comfortable than the castles had been.

Near the coast the houses were often built of flint, or of small stones from the sea-shore and from places where the sea had once been.

If you had lived in a forested district, your house would

Early medieval manor house

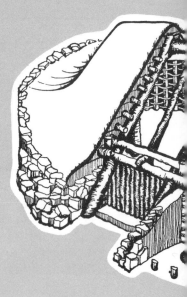

This shows how poor people made th

26

have had a wooden framework, with some kind of filling in between the wooden parts. In the simpler of these houses the framework consisted of two upright poles with a horizontal branch, called the "ridge", fixed from the top of one pole to the top of the other. Other branches leant against this ridge all round, and were called "rafters".)

The first improvement was to make upright ends by using strong curved "crucks" of oak, which supported the roof ridge and meant that the inconvenient poles no longer had to stand up in the middle of the floor. The crucks were arranged in pairs with their top ends meeting, rather like a letter A. The tops of these houses were too small and narrow for use as rooms, so there was no upstairs. If more room was wanted in the home, a lean-to shed could be built at one end of the house, but it was not possible to alter the main framework.

The spaces between the wooden framework were usually filled in with "wattle and daub".

This was made by fixing some flexible twigs, such as those of willow trees, upright into slots cut into the framework. These were called "wattles". Other twigs were then woven in and out of these upright ones, in the same way as you would make a basket, as you can see in the drawing.

When the space had been filled in with these woven twigs, a mixture of wet clay and chopped straw was spread, or "daubed", on both sides and it stuck to the wattles. Sometimes a top coat of lime plaster was added, sometimes the hair of animals, or even of people, was used to strengthen the clay instead of chopped straw. Later on bricks were used to fill the spaces. But the idea was always the same—to make a smooth, weather-proof covering to a house built with a wooden framework.

The roof was covered either with turf, or with a thatch of straw, and wattles had to be woven between the rafters to support this covering.

The ground inside the house was scooped out to give extra room for people to stand up. The soil that was dug up was piled round outside the hut, to prevent the ends of the rafters from slipping outwards. How do you prevent the poles of a tent from slipping outwards if you go camping now?

In one wall of such a house, a space would be left for an entrance, and it would have a rough wooden door, made in two parts, an upper and a lower one. The top part could be opened to let in light and air and the bottom closed to keep the pigs and chickens in the house in bad weather. Country people lived with their animals in their home with them, especially in winter.

One or two small openings were usually left in other walls to let light in, but there was no glass in these windows. Probably a piece of cloth or of animal skin would be fixed across them in very bad weather.

Simple houses such as these were built by families for themselves and not by skilled builders. Before two people could be married they had to build a house for themselves, probably with the help of friends and neighbours. You can be sure the children helped too, in many ways. It would be fun seeing the house grow and then visiting it later, when it was in use.

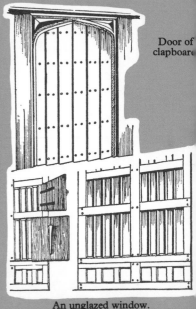

Door of clapboard

An unglazed window. You can see that shutters were hinged or sliding

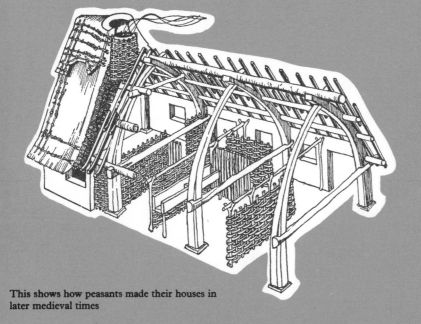

This shows how peasants made their houses in later medieval times

Larger, richer wooden houses were built in a different
way. They had an oak framework, joined together with large
oak pins. With these framed houses each floor was built on
a separate frame. In order that the upper floor should be
quite firm, the cross beams were laid right across the lower
frame, and jutted out beyond it. You can tell whether a
timber-framed house of this type is very old, by noticing
whether each storey does jut out beyond the one below it in
this way.

Older timber houses, built when wood was very plentiful,
have the uprights of the frame (called the studs) placed
closely together. Later on, when timber became scarce, the
studs were placed much further apart. This is another way
of telling whether a house is very old or not.

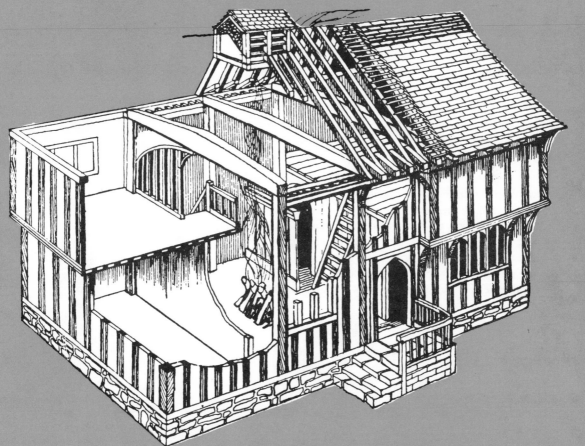

Late medieval yeoman's house showing central
hall, store with solar over, on left, and kitchen
with loft over, on right

Things to do and talk about

1 Old houses tell us a lot about the times in which they were built. You will be able to feel a little more what it was like to live in Britain in the Middle Ages if you can visit any of these houses.

Cornwall	Cotehele
Derbyshire	Haddon Hall
Devon	Bradley Manor
Gloucestershire	Horton Court
Kent	Penshurst Place
Lancashire	Ruffold Old Hall
Lincolnshire	Gainsborough Old Hall
Norfolk	Oxburgh Hall
Shropshire	Stokesay Castle
Somerset	Muchelney
Sussex	Alfriston Clergy House
Wiltshire	Great Chalfield Manor
Yorkshire	Shibden Hall
Wales	Bodrhyddan Hall

2 Begin a collection of guidebooks and postcards from houses you visit. It will grow very slowly, but you will get a lot of fun from comparing the different houses and their contents.

3 Notice the materials used in any medieval buildings you come across. Why do we find granite being used in Devon, limestone in the Cotswolds, timber and bricks in some areas, flint, or lath and clay in others?

Hospitals, almshouses, chantries, chapels, schools

4 Are there any medieval schools or colleges in your town? Many old towns have religious buildings other than parish churches (e.g. the Greyfriars Chapel in King's Lynn). Are there any almshouses or medieval hospitals in your town? This photograph shows the Leycester Hospital in Warwick. During the Middle Ages this was a guildhall. In 1571 it was converted into an almshouse.

4 Inside the home

Boys and girls in the Middle Ages were accustomed to homes that would seem to us now to be very uncomfortable. At first there were no separate rooms and everybody lived, ate and slept in the same room. If your family was wealthy the large room of the castle or manor house where you lived was called the hall. This had a raised platform, called the dais, at one end and at the other end a wooden partition, often with a gallery above it.

The main house of a village is sometimes still called "The Hall".

Homes of all kinds were very cold and dark and draughty in winter. Doors and window spaces were small and either open, or had poorly-fitting shutters and the only heating was by a wood fire like a bonfire in the middle of the floor. The smoke drifted about the room until it found a way out through a hole in the roof, or through the window openings. By the 15th century brick fireplaces were being built in new houses and the fire no longer had to be in the middle of the room.

The walls of the hall in a castle or manor house were often covered with brightly-coloured paintings on the bare plaster, like the walls of churches. The pictures were of scenes from bible stories or from well-known legends.

Later, those families which could afford them bought tapestries to hang on their walls. These are large cloths woven with pictures on them. They helped to keep out some of the draughts and were also convenient because they could be unhooked and taken away when you travelled about or moved to another home. Such tapestries were called "arras" because the best kinds were made in the town of Arras, in France.

Families which could not afford to buy arras sometimes hung plain woven cloth on their walls, with pictures painted on it, and those who were poorer still had to make do with the bare plaster. Perhaps you would have helped your father paint the plaster of your home to brighten it up in springtime.

Families were often large and the smaller homes must have been very crowded. The lord of a castle or of a large manor house also had a great many other people living in his home, as well as his wife and children. Every household had to support itself. There were very few shops even in such towns as existed then, and we have to remember that London itself was only like a large village. So you probably did not have to go on shopping errands then, as you do now, though you might sometimes have had to walk a very long way on some other kind of errand—perhaps to take a message or a present to someone living some way away. Certainly people could not rely, as they do nowadays, on a baker or grocer or butcher or postman calling at the door.

For these reasons a great many servants were necessary in a large household, and the people who lived in a castle or manor house were almost as many as would live now in a small village. (We must not think of a medieval household as being at all like a modern family.)

With so many people and so few rooms there could not have been any privacy in your home, whether you were rich or poor. But perhaps people did not notice, because they were used to living in that way. After all, most people could not read, and there was no radio or television to disturb you if you wanted to think quietly. Life was busy and noisy and lively, and to a boy or girl it must have been full of interest and excitement. There were always comings and goings, and talk and noise; we shall hear more about that when we consider what work people did, and how boys and girls helped the grown-ups.

Notice the later four poster bed

Fireplace with logs resting on andirons or firedogs

Thirteenth century chair, stools and fifteenth century form

Later in the Middle Ages, people began to be more concerned about comfort and quiet in their homes, and the hall was no longer the only room in a large household. Gradually, smaller rooms were added round the hall: a kitchen, a buttery and pantry, a sitting-room called a solar, and bedrooms. By about the 15th century, if you were a boy or girl of a well-to-do family, you might have had a bedroom to yourself. But there were also a great many families which had only small, one-roomed homes, for a long time yet, and even the grandest houses were very inconvenient.

There was very little furniture, even in the larger houses. Chairs were very rare and only the head of the household, or an important guest, had one to sit on. Other grown-ups, and all boys and girls, had to make do with wooden stools or benches. These did not have backs to them and must have been very uncomfortable. Well-to-do families had cushions to put on their furniture.

A very usual kind of seating was a fixed bench, made as a part of the framework of the walls. This was really just a ledge jutting out and was often very narrow.

Tables were at first rough wooden trestles, made to be taken down when a meal was finished. Later, they were made solidly, and not so that they could be taken apart. In grand houses tables were sometimes very long, so that all the important guests at a banquet could sit down together. In well-to-do homes they were always covered with linen cloths. On these were set out spoons and knives, cups and jugs of wood and of earthenware.

Forks were not known in England until very much later. It was the custom to display gold and silver vessels on your table, if you had them, and on the cupboards, which were at first just small shelves on which you placed the cups.

Plates, even in wealthy houses, were often of wood, and frequently meat was eaten on trenchers, or thick slices of bread, which were afterwards given to the poor or flung on to the floor for the dogs.

Clothes were kept at first on pegs and rods hammered into the wall, or in a chest.

Chests were the most common household possession for many centuries. They were at first wooden boxes made of six boards nailed and pegged together—four for the sides and one each for the bottom and the lid. This was a very simple piece of furniture to make and probably every household had at least one chest. If your father was wealthy he probably had several, and some of them would be richly carved.

This chest with its lid fixed has become a side-table. The front is pierced to make a food cupboard

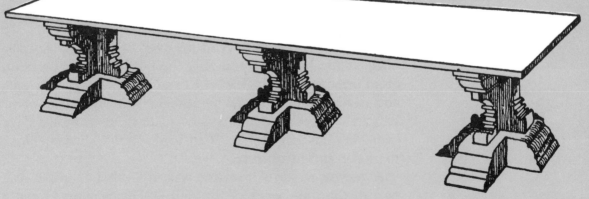

Trestle table

34

Fourteenth century chest which has become a cupboard. It has wrought iron hinges and mounts

Thirteenth century chest with carved roundels

A simple chest of six boards

Chests were used for all sorts of purposes. They were, as we have said, useful for storing clothes and also for keeping tools in, as well as armour and other valuable possessions. Many chests had locks which were opened by heavy iron keys. If you travelled about you used a chest as we now use a suitcase, to take your belongings with you. And they were also used to sit on and to lie down on and could be quickly packed and carried off in times of danger.

Later, various kinds of cupboards gradually took the place of chests—plate cupboards, for keeping tableware in, and small cupboards called aumbries, with their doors perforated with carving, for keeping food in.

Your toys and other belongings would probably have been piled in a corner—or left lying about, for there were so few pieces of furniture that it is unlikely that children had anywhere of their own to keep their things in.

You can be sure that boys and girls were not allowed to use the best furniture either, when there was so little of any of it. You would have been accustomed to being uncomfortable, but as you didn't know of any other way of living, you probably did not think about it.

Another necessary piece of furniture in a medieval home was a cradle. Cradles were made of wood, plain or carved according to who made them and often they had a hood to keep out the draughts, and rockers. If you had younger brothers and sisters you might have spent quite a lot of time looking after them and rocking them in their cradles.

Older children slept on the floor among the rushes. It must have been pleasant to fall asleep by the light of the fire, watching the shadows playing on the decorated walls, and listening to the grown-ups chatting.

Even grown-ups slept on the floor, or on very rough wooden bedsteads, without any kind of springs but with the mattress resting on ropes which passed through holes in the wooden framework of the bed. Poorer people had no beds at all, but slept on rough bags filled with straw and covered themselves with anything they could find. Often a shaped piece of wood was used as a pillow, or a cloak or cover would be doubled up for one. A box filled with straw was probably one of the first ideas for sleeping warmly and more comfortably. Then, if someone thought of packing the straw into a thick bag so that it did not feel so prickly, they had a mattress for their bed. Very grand beds had a roof, called a "tester", and curtains hung down from this. The curtains were drawn round the bed at night, but in the daytime they were often tied up into bags and used for keeping things in. Later, the tester was supported on posts at the four corners and people no longer used the curtains as furniture!

When houses were draughty and cold it must have seemed very cosy behind the curtains, but probably some boys and girls still preferred to sleep out in the open, by the fire, so that they could watch all that was going on before they fell asleep.

Thirteenth century baby's cradle

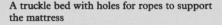

A truckle bed with holes for ropes to support the mattress

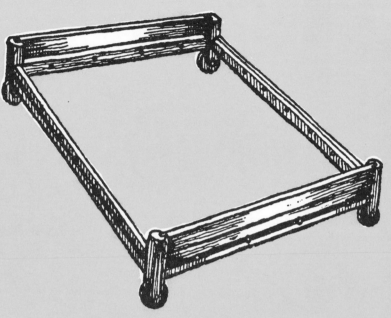

A grand bed

When grown-ups had proper beds, children and servants often slept on small, low beds, called truckle or trundle beds. These were pushed—trundled—under a bigger bed during the daytime. They had small wheels fixed under the wooden framework and at night the truckle was pulled out and made up ready for sleeping. In the morning it was put away again. It was probably good fun to slide to and fro on a truckle bed!

Beds were so rare and valuable that people sometimes left them in their wills to their friends. In the 15th century there was a well-to-do family called Paston, living in Norfolk. We know a good deal about them because they wrote a great many letters to one another and many of these have been preserved and still exist. When Margaret Paston, wife of a wealthy landowner, died in 1484, she had made a will leaving her possessions to her children and her friends, and she made special mention of several beds. One of her sons got a feather-bed which was a great treasure because it was so rare. Another bed went to a daughter, together with two curtains to hang round it, and several woollen blankets.

As we have aid, medieval rooms were much darker than ours are today. For artificial light the poorer homes used rush-lights, or else managed with the light of the fire. In large households candles or oil-burning lamps, called cressets, were used.

Rushlights were made from the stalks of the rush-plants which grows on wet marshy ground. In autumn you and the other children would have been sent to gather armfuls of rushes, to be dried in the sun, or indoors if it were wet weather. When the stalks were dry, some of them were used for strewing on the stone or mud floor, others for making rushlights. They were peeled, except for a strip down one side, which was left to keep the rush stiff. They were then cut into lengths of about a foot and dipped several times into hot melted fat. Bacon fat was thought to be the best kind for making rushlights and we shall read later on how the fat was collected when mother was cooking the joint.

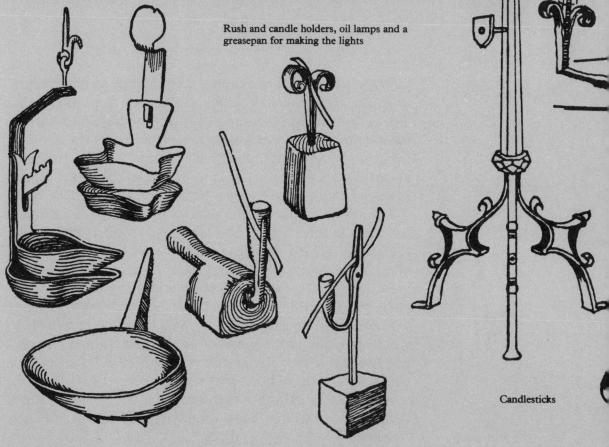

Rush and candle holders, oil lamps and a greasepan for making the lights

Candlesticks

Lanterns: two are pierced and two have windows of horn or glass

If you examine the stem of a rush, you will see that the inside is spongy, so that it readily sucked up the fat. After each dipping the "rush" was left to dry so that each new layer of fat stuck on to the one underneath, until the rush stalk looked very much like a modern taper.

Rushlights were lit from the fire and placed in holders, called "nips", because they were rather like forceps at the end, and nipped the rush. A rushlight gave a faint, flickering light and lasted for about half an hour.

Candles were also made at home, by dipping wicks into melted wax so that they were often called "dips", but for a long time they were only used by wealthy people. Candlesticks were made of iron and many of them were jointed, so that they could be extended, to give a better light. Even wealthy homes must have been very dimly lit, but people did not mind that as much as we should, for most of them could not read or write, and they usually went to bed when it got dark, and got up at daybreak.

A lantern made from a candle stuck into a metal frame, with horn sides, was used for carrying about. A lantern was often called a "lant*horn*".

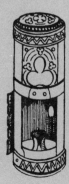

Things to do and talk about

1 Make a list of ways in which a grand medieval home was different from an ordinary one.

2 Why did people in the Middle Ages go to bed much earlier than we do, especially in winter? Imagine you are a boy or girl lying awake in bed; what would you see and think about?

3 Make models in cardboard of a grand bed, a child's bed in a grand house and a poor person's bed.

4 Study this picture and try to answer the questions.

What is the purpose of the graduated spit above the fire?
What kind of book do you think the lady is reading?

5 Helping at home

IF you start to make a list of all the things you eat, wear and use at home, you will find that they are nearly all provided for you by somebody outside your family. In the Middle Ages all these things had to be made at home, and boys and girls often helped.

Cooking was much more complicated than it is now, and much more interesting. Of course, nothing could be bought in packets or tins and mother had to see that fruits, vegetables, and other perishable foods were preserved when they were fresh so that they could be used in winter-time. You might have been given the job of putting layers of salt in between layers of vegetables in a large earthenware jar, or of heating and stirring the honey that the fruit was to be kept in.

Many dishes were richly seasoned with herbs grown in home gardens and with spices which were brought to Europe from the East. Vinegar was used in nearly all dishes, and flowers too. Roses, violets and cowslips were crystallized, or cooked slowly in honey, and made a delicious sweetmeat for special occasions.

There was nothing to feed farm animals on in winter-time, when the grass was not growing, for root-crops, such as turnips, were unknown in England. So the animals were mostly killed in the autumn and the meat had to be salted to keep it good to eat and it was richly seasoned in cooking, to make it less monotonous.

Almost the only fresh meat eaten in winter was pigeon and other smaller birds. Many people kept pigeon-houses and dovecots near their homes. The birds became half tame but fed themselves on wild berries, seeds and so on. We often read of a poacher stealing a pigeon for his wife to put into a pie.

In every household, except the poorest, wine and ale were made and the children probably helped to make it from the fruits and flowers they had gathered, and from barley. Bread had to be baked at home, too, and was darker and rougher than modern white bread—and much more nourishing.

Many people living in towns sent a good deal of their food to the cook-shops, where pies, puddings and baked meats could be prepared from your own ingredients. Except in families where there were plenty of servants, the boys and girls probably went to and from the cook-shops. There, you could either buy a dish of hot food ready for eating, or take the family joint in to be cooked. Here is what it cost to cook various dishes at a cook-shop in London in the 14th century:

"The best roast pig for 8d. Three roast thrushes 2d. Ten eggs, one penny. For the paste, fire and trouble upon a goose, 2d." (You took your own goose.)

In large houses in medieval times the kitchen was often a little apart, connected with the main house by a covered passage. This was because when houses were built mainly of wood there was a great risk of sparks from the kitchen fire setting light to the rest of the house. Gradually, as more of the larger houses were built of brick or stone, the kitchen came to be planned as a part of the house, as it is now.

The implements needed for cooking were made by hand, either at home or by the local smith or carpenter. Pots had to be very solid to stand up to being used on a large open fire, and so they were very heavy to lift. Cooking a dinner for a large family must have been much more tiring in early times than it is now. Since food took much longer to cook and a wood fire is likely to die down suddenly, you might often have been expected to watch both the fire and the cooking.

The earliest kind of cooking-vessel was an iron pot or cauldron, often with three legs and looking rather like a circular coal-scuttle. This could stand by the fire, or even right over the top of it, without falling over. It was used chiefly for stewing meat and for making soups and broths which people enjoyed very much.

Killing, cutting up and salting the winter meat supply

Medieval cooking implements: cooking pot, shears and scissors, spoon, knife, hanging pot and flesh hook, cauldron and skillet

Later, somebody thought of arranging things so that the cauldrons could be hung over the fire by an iron rod. This rod had an attachment at the top by which it could be put over an iron bar running across the chimney opening. Sometimes several pots would hang from one of these chimney bars, and some of them could be raised or lowered on notched bars. So mother could push her pot of stew up or down over the heat, instead of turning the gas down or up under the saucepan as she does nowadays!

Another kind of pan used for boiling was a skillet, a little three-legged saucepan with a long handle. The name "saucepan" was used for any kind of small pan, like a skillet, suitable for making sauce in.

In larger kitchens the fire was large enough and hot enough for a good deal of the family cooking to be done in front of it. One of the most general ways of doing this was on a spit.

This was a long metal rod with a point at one end and a handle at the other. The point was stuck through a joint of meat and the two ends rested on little hooks on the side of the fire-dogs nearest to the fire. There are several different kinds of spit, as you can see in the drawings.

Of course, a spit had to be kept turning, or else one side of the joint would burn and the other side would not be cooked at all. Turning the spit was a favourite job which mother would get the children to do. In wealthy households a small boy was employed as a "turnspit".

To turn the spit you had to sit by the fire, on the floor or on a low stool, and turn an iron handle which moved the spit round and so turned the meat over and over. We still talk of a joint being "done to a turn" nowadays.

"Dripping" was the name given to the fat which dripped from the joint into a long narrow pan which stood under the spit. The meat was basted with the dripping from time to time, and when the cooking was done it was kept for making lights.

Later in the Middle Ages, spits were made which could be worked by a dog, and later still they were worked by clockwork.

When the spits had been used they were, of course, very greasy and had to be cleaned. This was another of the jobs which you might be told to do, and mother would have expected you to polish the metal till it shone brightly. The spits were kept on a wooden spit-rack which was on the wall over the fireplace.

A straight spit on a spitrack, a pronged spit,
a basket spit

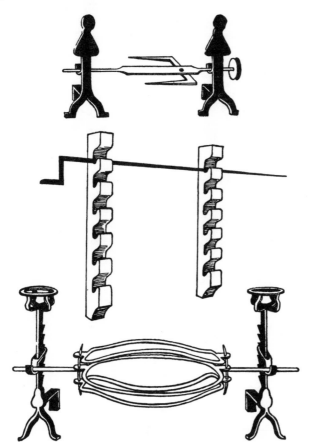

For cleaning there were, of course, no packets of soap powder or tins of polish. The spit, the metal pots and pans, candlesticks, tankards and bowls were all cleaned with fine sand, sifted ashes and linseed oil. Small mops made of bunches of heather and brooms of birch or willow twigs (which bend easily) were used for what little house-cleaning was done. They were much like the brooms made of twigs which are still used nowadays to sweep up leaves in gardens.

Most people did not bother much about keeping themselves clean. In better-class houses there was usually a small table in the bedroom, on which stood a metal basin and jug. Books of etiquette, or manners, were read in wealthy families. One of the rules written there was that children must wash their faces, hands and teeth every morning.

But simpler people washed very little and nobody at all thought of having baths regularly. Many people believed that nobody should ever have one unless their doctor ordered it!

Here are 15th century instructions to a servant when preparing a bath for his master when he is not well:

"Boil together hollyhock, mallow, wall pellitory, and brown fennel, danewort, St. John's wort, centuary, ribwort and camomile, heyhove, hayriff, herbbenet, bresewort, smallage, water speedwell, scabious, bugloss and wild flax which is good for aches—boil withy leaves and great oats together with them, and throw them into a vessel and put your lord over it and let him endure it for a while as hot as he can, being covered over and closed on every side; and whatever disease, grievance or pain ye be vexed with, this medicine shall surely make you whole, as men say."

The chief job that your mother and the other women living in your home—aunts, older sisters, and so on—had to do was spinning. All the thread used for weaving cloth was spun in private houses. Because the unmarried women had time to do a good deal of the spinning, they came to be called "spinsters". Nowadays the word is used to describe any woman who is not married, although of course she no longer does any spinning—except perhaps for fun.

Basting roasting birds on a spit

Bird roasting on a spit. Notice the turnspit whose face is protected by a wet straw target, the drip-pan to catch the grease and a cauldron on a ratchet

At first spinning was done on a distaff, and only later on a spinning-wheel. A distaff was a wooden rod. On one end a rough mass of sheep's wool was fastened and a little of this was drawn out at a time and twisted between finger and thumb to form a thread, which was wound on to the spindle.

Every woman had her own distaff—and most girls too. Sometimes we read that they were used as weapons, when there was a quarrel in the family!

Weaving was a heavier job and was usually done by men, with boys helping to work the looms. Silk weaving on small, light looms was a job for the women and girls. Rich and splendid silks, satins and velvets which were worn by wealthy people were usually imported from the East, but small silk objects such as ribbons and girdles were woven by "silk-women" and girls who helped them.

Women carding in two ways, spinning wool and weaving cloth

A girl spinning, others weaving on a treadle loom and a tapestry loom

There were very few doctors in the Middle Ages and many medicines were made at home. Herbs were much used for these. Some of the remedies seem to us to be absurd, such as putting a wreath of the plant pennyroyal round your head as a cure for headache or giddiness, and rubbing raw onion on to a bite caused by a mad dog! Many other cures were more sensible, such as drinking an infusion of camomile to cure a fever.

Almost nothing was known about the causes of illness and a great many children died young. Although families were large, the boys and girls seldom all grew up. We sometimes find a medieval tomb which has on it the figures of a husband and wife and of all their children, living and dead. The dead are shown lying down, the living are standing in a row.

If boys or girls managed to keep healthy and well in the Middle Ages, they must have lived happily and had a great deal of fun, but if they became ill for any reason they were not very likely to get better. There were no hospitals or clinics, no health service and no public health laws to compel people to give proper care to cleanliness in food or water, to drainage or to sanitation.

Things to do and talk about

1 Draw the important utensils your mother uses in her cooking, and alongside each one draw what she would have used in the Middle Ages.

2 Find out how a dress or shirt was obtained in the Middle Ages.

3 Make a list of the materials used in the clothes you are wearing, and compare them with the clothes of a medieval boy or girl.

4 Describe and illustrate a day in your life as it would be if you were a servant in a medieval manor house.

5 Here are some of the things you could buy at two shops in the Middle Ages. How many can you still buy today?

GOODS ON SALE

Cook Shop	*Pasties :*	**Haberdashers:**
Roast meats :	capon pie	caps
lamb	goose pie	shirts
goose	chicken pie	thread
pork		purses
chicken		combs
rabbit		nightcaps
duck		girdles
lark		cord
partridge		socks
pigeon		beads
woodcock		cushions
thrush		ribbon
heron		hats
pheasant		hoods
capon		laces

6 Helping on the Manor

IF you had been playing in the fields near your home one sunny day in the summer of 1085, you might have seen a small group of horsemen riding up to the manor house. They might then have come and questioned your father, and other men in the village, and there would be much gossip and excitement before it was known just what these strange men had come for.

They were officers who had come from King William, to call the lord of the manor of each district, and some of the villages from each manor, to attend the local court and answer questions about the countryside. You will remember that William of Normandy and his followers had defeated the Saxons under King Harold at the Battle of Hastings in 1066.

William wanted to rule England well and this, of course, would cost a lot of money, so he needed to know how much land people owned and how much they could afford to pay him in taxes. So he sent his officers round asking questions like these: Who owns this manor? How big is it? How many people live on it? How many oxen are there? How many ploughs? How many horses? How many pigs? How much woodland? How many fishponds are there? Is there a mill? and so on.

The nobles did not like answering these questions and sometimes they did not tell the truth. When the officers thought that this was so, they called certain of the villagers and asked them what they thought the facts were. And so anyone might, at any time during that summer, have been asked about his district and from all the varied answers that people gave, the truth was arrived at.

All the facts were written down, and when the men got back to London everything they had found out was put together into a book, called Domesday Book. This book is still in London, in the Public Record Office. It is written

A small boy holds the horse
while it is shod

in Latin, in black and red ink, and it tells us about every village and town in England at the time it was written. It is quite possible that the place where you live is mentioned in Domesday Book, even though it may not be as important now as it was then.

Nearly everybody in England in the Middle Ages possessed some land. King William had given his Norman barons large estates. In return the barons had to promise that they would fight for William when he wanted their help, and bring soldiers for his army. They also had to pay him sums of money and come to his court to seek justice when any injury had been done them, or when they themselves had broken any of William's laws.

Some of the nobles had so much land given to them that they gave some of it to their own followers, who made the same promises to them that they had made to the king.

The large estates were formed into manors. A manor consisted of a village and the land round about it, on which its inhabitants worked. The manor house was where the lord of the manor lived, with his family and servants. It was a farm as well as a home, and it was also a court of law to which people brought their disputes and their complaints.

Harrowing and weeding

The ordinary villagers were called villeins. Each villein had several strips of land in various parts of the big open fields of the manor. He did not own his land or his cottage, but was allowed to use them on condition that he did two or three days' work each week on the lord's fields. So you see, your life would have been very different according to whether you lived in the manor house or in a villein's cottage.

Besides doing work for him, the villeins had to serve the lord in other ways. At harvest time they had to do extra work and they also had to give the lord a certain amount of the food they produced on their own land—chickens and geese, perhaps, and eggs and fish. They had to take their corn to the lord's mill to be ground into flour and he charged them heavily for grinding it. They often had to pay for for being allowed to put their sheep and pigs to graze on the lord's land, too. They were not allowed to leave the manor without the lord's permission and they also had to ask his consent before their children could get married.

Ploughing, breaking clods and sowing

The only way in which a villein could free himself was by running away to a town and hiding there. If he was not brought back within a year and a day, he was a free man and could settle down anywhere where he could find a lord who would give him a home and some land. Or he could get work in a town.

Gradually the custom arose of allowing a villein to buy himself out of service. That is, he could pay the lord a sum of money instead of working for him. With this money the lord could hire labourers and pay them wages. This pleased the lord, for he probably found that it was better to have workmen he paid, instead of those who were forced to work for him. It suited the villein, too, because he had more free time to look after his own land, and it suited the poorer ones who needed money more than they needed time off. By the end of the Middle Ages most farmers were "free men", earning wages for their work and paying rent for their house and land.

There were of course no large towns and no factories in the Middle Ages, so that nearly everybody lived in the country and earned their living in some way from the land. The English countryside looked very different then. Each farmer had a certain number of narrow strips of land, like long allotments. These strips were scattered over the open fields between those of neighbours, so that everyone had his fair share of good and of poor land. There were no hedges round the fields and divisions were made by piling up ridges of turf between one person's strip of land and the next. But as time went on people found it convenient to exchange strips so as to have their land in one piece and hedges were planted round it. There were a lot of forests and some of the land did not belong to anybody, but was called common land. We still use the word "common" to mean a piece of land which anybody can use.

One of the jobs which quite young children often had to do was to take the animals to the common land and keep an eye on them while they grazed. There are many drawings in medieval manuscripts showing boys and girls looking after cows, sheep and geese.

Because several people's animals might be grazing all together, it was necessary to have some way of knowing which were which. Each animal had to be marked to show who was its owner, and if it were found straying without anyone to attend to it, it was put into an enclosed piece of ground, with a fence round it, which was called a "pound". The owner had to pay a small fine to get his animal out of the pound, as you probably have to pay a penny to get something out of "lost property" at school. If you had gone off to play and let the animals stray, no doubt you would have got into trouble at home.

Sometimes villagers stole animals which had been put into the pound. Here is an entry in the proceedings of a manor court in the 14th century: "Margaret and Alice Otes broke the lord's pound for 4 pigs taken for a debt to the lord. Fine 6d."

And here is another entry, relating to the same village: "William, of the household of Matilda Charle, made an illegal path over the land of the lord at Walsinghamgate with a cart. Fine 3d."

Cutting, stacking and carting the corn

Growing crops was work which boys and girls could help with. There are pictures in the Luttrell Psalter, a famous fourteenth century manuscript, which give us an idea of all the jobs which had to be done. The land was turned over by oxen yoked to wooden ploughs. Someone had to walk behind the plough, breaking up the larger clods of earth with wooden mallets; then a harrow, very much like the ones pulled behind tractors nowadays, was used to break up the earth into still finer pieces. Sowing seed was done by throwing it by hand to and fro as you walked along. There was weeding to be done while the crops were growing, and scaring away the birds that might eat the seed or the ripe corn was a job which children enjoyed. You might have a sling, or just loose stones to throw, and you probably had to shout and sing as well. The ripe corn was cut with a small sickle, and tied into bundles by hand. The sheaves were stacked by hand and in the winter-time the corn was threshed.

Threshing means separating the grain from the chaff and stalks. The wheat, rye, barley or oats was spread out on the floor of a barn and hit hard with a flail. This is a wooden club, made in two parts which are hinged together with pieces of leather. It must have been great fun to help with the threshing; as you hit the heads of corn with the flail the grains came tumbling out, and probably you sometimes hit someone nearby by mistake—or even on purpose! The chaff was blown away by shaking a sack or a straw mat, or something of that kind, over the grains. The grains of corn were then gathered up, taken to the mill and ground into flour. Barley was not usually ground, but was made into malt and used for brewing ale, which was the usual drink. Tea and coffee were not introduced until very much later.

When the harvest had been gathered in, the animals were turned on to the fields to manure them and to pick up what food they could before the ground was ploughed again in November. "Harvest Home" in the autumn was a time for much feasting and jollification.

Everyone worked hard and there was little time for play, but there was always a good deal going on and most boys and girls probably enjoyed sharing in the work of the manor. There were holidays, too; the lord could not make the villeins work on Sundays or on the great church festivals. They were not allowed to work on their own land then either.

Keeping and tending the flocks

Many poor families added to what food they could grow, by poaching from the lord's land. Fish from his fishponds, pigeons from his pigeon-house and rabbits and pheasants snared from his woods were tasty and worth a risk to get. If you were caught you were whipped, or spent a day in the stocks, and an account of what you had done was written on the roll (or list) of the manor court. If anyone committed a serious crime, such as shooting one of the lord's deer, he was outlawed. This meant that he must leave the country altogether and never come back. If he was found again he could be killed. Sometimes an outlaw did not leave the country, but hid himself and lived as best he could, like Robin Hood, who lived in Sherwood Forest.

There were all sorts of fetching-and-carrying jobs which boys and girls helped to do, when they were not busy with something else. You might be sent down to the stream

Threshing with flails and taking ground flour from the mill

to collect rushes for use in the house, or reeds for thatching the buildings. When your father went with a horse and cart to fetch salt from somewhere by the sea—or from somebody else who had collected it—you probably went with him and the trip would be interesting. There might be farm produce to be taken to market in the nearest town and other things to buy there.

April was always a particularly busy month in the dairy, for then milk was very plentiful and quantities of butter and cheese had to be made. Boys and girls could take a turn at the tiring work of churning. People also liked ewes' milk for their cheese then.

One of the changes that came about during the Middle Ages was that horses were used more and more for ploughing instead of oxen. You might have heard many arguments between your father and his friends as to which was best. Here is a thirteenth-century writer's view:

"The plough of oxen is better than the plough of hors but (unless) yf it be upon stony groune ye whiche greveth sore the oxen in theyr fete. And ye plough of hors is more costly than ye plough of oxen and yet shal your plough of oxen doo as moche werke in a yere as youre plough of hors though ye dryve your hors faster than ye do your oxen. . . ."

Things to do and talk about

1 Make a Country Calendar, with one page to each month and draw or paste pictures on it to show what was done or grown.

2 Implements used in farming changed slowly. You may be able to find in a museum some that are very like medieval ones, although they were made later.

3 Visit a farm and make drawings to show how it is different from a medieval one.

4 Make a list of what a peasant had to do in return for his cottage and some land.

5 The illustration shows peasants at work. Describe briefly what each is doing.

7 Helping in the town

A walled town

As we have seen, few towns in the Middle Ages were larger than a modern village. Most of the houses had gardens of their own and even if you lived in London you had a garden and did not have to walk for many minutes before you were outside the city walls and in open country. Pigs, geese and chickens roamed about in most towns, though in London in the 14th century any found wandering about the streets were forfeited. So there was plenty of excitement for boys and girls living in towns.

Most towns had walls round them to protect the people from danger; gates in the walls were shut at night time and if you awoke you would have heard the watchman on his rounds calling out the hours all through the night.

A walled garden in a town

People were proud of belonging to a particular town. Nowadays, if you live in Durham or Exeter or Margate, you think of yourself first of all as being English, but children, and grown-ups too, used to be brought up to think of themselves as "a citizen of Durham"—or Exeter, or whatever town they lived in. This is really not surprising for, as we have seen, a great many people never in their whole lives visited any other part of the country but the district they were born in. People were always on the watch to protect their own customs, their trade and their homes and there was sometimes even fighting between the people of two different towns, over such things.

Many towns were ruled by a corporation—people chosen by the townsfolk to arrange their affairs—and the mayor who was their chairman or leader. They made laws for everyone in the town and had to see that they were obeyed. If the laws were broken the person concerned was tried in the court of the town and punished in some suitable way. A little later on we shall see some of the kinds of things that people did wrong, and how they were punished.

Within the walls of the city, craftsmen of every kind had

their shops. The things sold in the shops were usually made by the man who sold them, so when you went to buy anything you saw the master and his apprentices working. As a rule each trade kept to its own street or district. You may be interested to discover whether there are any street-names like Weavers' Row, or Goldsmiths' Street, near your home.

Most boys living in towns in medieval times learned a trade by being apprenticed to a master of that trade. When you were about fourteen your father would arrange for you to go to learn a trade. It was not easy to get taken on by a good master without special recommendation from some-body.

An agreement was made between you and your new master. You had to promise to be a good, hard-working and obedient pupil, and not to waste your master's time, or his possessions. The master had to promise to teach you his trade, to keep you as one of his household, to feed and clothe you and to beat you if you needed it! Girls were put as apprentices, too, to such trades as embroidery.

You were apprenticed to a master craftsman for seven years, and your father paid a "premium" to him. Some-times this was paid by instalments. In 1275 a mother agreed to pay for the apprenticeship of her son William, in four equal sums. If a master did not do what was agreed, he had to return the sum that had been paid to him.

Shopping

Buying fish

Most apprentices were treated as one of the family, but some masters were very harsh. Some boys hated their work and left as soon as they could, and some ran away. One boy, called Simon Eyre, had a very strange experience; he served his master for seven years before he discovered that he was working for a master upholsterer, and not for a master draper as he had thought! Simon managed to find a master draper who took him on after that and he did so well under him that he became rich and prosperous and was Lord Mayor of London some years later.

Richard, or "Dick", Whittington was the son of a country gentleman in Gloucestershire, and was apprenticed to a London mercer. This was a man who made cloth. As we know from the story, Dick nearly gave up trying to settle as an apprentice in London, but changed his mind and did very well. He, too, became Lord Mayor of London.

At the end of your apprenticeship you would have had to pass a kind of exam, though not a written one as you do at school now. You had to show how skilful you were, by making a "master-piece"—a piece of furniture, or a window-frame perhaps, if you were apprenticed to a carpenter, a specially nice gold bowl or jug if you were apprenticed to a goldsmith, or a fine pair of shoes if your master was a shoemaker. If your piece was good enough you could then be a "master" yourself.

When you had finished your apprenticeship you usually got a job working for another master for some time, and were paid wages as a workman is today. You were called a journeyman, or *journée*-man, which in French meant a man who worked by the day, for daily wages. While you were working as a journeyman you probably saved as much of your wages as you could, because you wanted to become a master on your own and that cost a lot of money. You had to buy a shop and the tools you needed and materials for making your goods.

Even when you had saved up enough money, you could not become a master craftsman until you were allowed to by the Guild of your particular craft. A guild was a society of all the men in a town who had the same trade. There was a goldsmiths' guild, a shoemakers' guild, a girdle-makers' guild, and so on. Inspectors of the guild came round to see that the masters were treating their apprentices well, that they were using good materials for their work and were selling their finished article for the fair price that the guild had fixed. Every member of a guild felt ashamed if a fellow-member produced a shoddy piece of work.

The inspectors also made sure that the apprentices had enough to eat, and that they were not made to work by candlelight. Can you think why this was considered wrong? (It was not because anybody thought that it was bad for the apprentices' eyesight.)

If you happened to be working for an unkind or dishonest master you would probably find an opportunity to tell the guild officers about it when they came round.

The guilds also helped any members who were too ill to work and looked after their widows and children when they died.

Because the guild inspectors were usually strict and because people were so proud of their own town, they were very particular about how shopkeepers behaved and there were all kinds of punishments when people cheated, as sometimes they did.

Often the punishment was made to fit the crime and boys and girls would have found it rather fun to watch. A dealer who had sold bad wine was compelled to drink some of it and had the rest poured over his head in public. A man who had used the public water supply when he had no right to do so was led through the streets with a leaky bucket of water on his head. A butcher who sold bad meat had to stand in the pillory and have his meat burnt in front of him, so that he could smell it for a long time. A weaver who was caught stretching his cloth to make it measure more, was put in the stocks, and so on.

Certain bakers in London were caught cheating their customers who brought dough to be baked. They kept a

A baker's shop

A punishment for selling short-weight loaves

small boy underneath the counter and when the customer put the dough down, the boy opened a little trap door and removed some of the dough from underneath. This the baker either used for himself, or sold to other people. The punishment for this kind of fraud was for the baker to be pulled through the streets of the town on a cart with a loaf of bread hung round his neck, for everyone to laugh at.

And there is a record of a boy called Robert Porter, the servant of a baker at Stratford, near London, who was cheating customers and was caught by the guild inspectors. He had been putting an iron weight into penny loaves of bread which were of short weight. Robert owned up when he was brought before the Mayor and Aldermen at the Guildhall in London. He was put in the pillory where he had to remain for an hour, with the loaf and a piece of iron round his neck. Perhaps he was only given an hour because he was young.

People who drank too much were often made to walk through the streets inside a barrel, as a punishment for being drunk.

Company in the stocks

There was great danger from fire in medieval towns. The streets were very narrow; the houses were built of wood and covered with thatch, so naturally they burnt easily. Most of the towns had fires from time to time which destroyed nearly all the buildings.

There was no fire-brigade and children as well as grown-ups had to help put out a fire with water drawn from wells or a river and carried in leather or wooden buckets. Usually the quickest way of stopping a fire when once it started was by pulling down the houses so as to prevent it from spreading, and special hooks and ropes had to be kept in every part of the town for this purpose. Once the first danger was past, you would probably have enjoyed throwing water on to the fire and dodging out of the way of bits of falling timber—though it would have been very hot and dusty work.

As time went on, laws were passed about what kinds of houses could be put up. By the beginning of the 13th century, new houses in London had to be roofed with tiles, though at Norwich thatched roofs were not forbidden until the 16th century. Such things depended upon what the people thought and what the Mayor and Alderman did about it.

In some towns there was a simple kind of water system. Water was collected from springs on high ground nearby and sent through wooden or earthenware pipes. The first water main, or "conduit", of this kind was installed in London in the 13th century and was intended for water for the poor to drink and for the wealthy people to cook their food with. Probably fetching water from a well or pump in the street was a job that you would often have to do if you lived in London then.

Another type of well

No kind of drainage system existed in London in the Middle Ages. Great houses had their own sanitation if they had any flowing water nearby, but most people threw their filth and garbage of all kinds into the streets, where there was an open trough along the middle, called a "midden". It was all left there until someone made a fuss and then it was carted away and dumped into the river or some other convenient place. The streets must have been very unpleasant and unhealthy and it is not surprising that there

Drawing water from the well

were frequent outbreaks of plague and other diseases.

Perhaps you have seen a pair of pattens. They were something like sandals raised up on a small iron hoop, so as to keep you and your shoes out of the worst of the filth when you walked about the streets.

You might sometimes have seen grand ladies walking along on their pattens, sniffing at "pomanders" so that they would not notice the smells. A pomander was often made from an orange, with cloves stuck into it. You yourself would probably just have had to put up with the smells and usually would not have noticed them much.

Most towns had a fair once a year and this was a very exciting time for everyone living in the town and in the country round about. "Foreigners" from other districts were welcomed and had to pay a toll, or subscription, to the lord of the manor or the corporation of the town for permission to trade at the fair. If you and your friends had nothing better to do, you perhaps went round the fair picking out the "foreigners" and possibly laughing and jeering unkindly at their strange clothes and speech—even though they might be Englishmen from only a few miles away.

A fair might be for only a few days, or an important one lasting for as long as three weeks. Everyone had saved up beforehand and took the opportunity of buying anything they needed, which they could not easily make at home or buy from local shops. They had to lay up enough stocks to last for a whole year: almonds, raisins and currants from the East, furs and velvets and more ordinary things like salt for pickling, tar, wine, and so on. A fair was a great event and there were amusements and entertainments of all kinds, as well as the stalls and the salesmen and the crowds of spectators.

A smelly drain

Things to do and talk about

1 Perhaps your town is one that existed in the Middle Ages. If so, it will have changed a lot. You could trace an outline map of the town today and draw on it any medieval buildings which are still there.

2 Look carefully at roofs and notice their shape and what materials they are made of. Are there any medieval ones?

3 Very few people could read in the Middle Ages and so all trades had to have a symbol of their own. Look at Inn signs and see if any in your district seem to have any connection with the Middle Ages.

4 **Look at the street names in your town.**
Try to find out which names describe past trades or crafts. Sometimes the names are obvious (e.g. Haymarket, Baker Street) and sometimes they are obscure (e.g. Petty Cury—'the little cookery'). Sometimes they are named after crafts which are no longer common or after names which are not normally used (e.g. Webster Row—'weaver row', or Mercer Street—'merchant street'). Sometimes the street names recall old buildings, fields, common land or woodland.

Here is a picture of builders at work. Can you tell what each man is doing?

8 Education

Boys and girls were brought up much more strictly in the Middle Ages than they are nowadays. They were expected to obey their parents in everything, to sit still and to be silent when grown-ups were about. There were continual family quarrels and many children were cruelly treated, though often in ways that were not considered cruel then. Their parents beat them frequently and their teachers did the same. Agnes Paston, in the 15th century, was so angry with her elder daughter who refused to marry the man chosen for her that she "beat her once in the week or twice, and sometimes twice on a day, and her head broke in two or three places".

And when a student at Cambridge University took his examination to become a Master of Grammar, he was given a birch stick and told to show the examiners how hard he could beat a boy who was brought in for the purpose. The boy was given 4d. (2p) afterwards!

There were very few schools and the few that existed were mostly connected with the church. Some of these had been founded by King Alfred the Great, in the 9th century.

Latin was the language of the Christian Church in the Middle Ages and educated people in most parts of Europe spoke French. William the Conqueror made a law that all teaching in England should be in Norman-French. This meant, therefore, that an English boy or girl not only had to learn Latin, but had first of all to learn the strange language in which the Latin lesson was given!

It meant, too, that ordinary people could not usually read and understand proclamations sent out by the king, however important they might be. Gradually, however, English became the language of both rich and poor people, as it had been before the Normans came. It was not until the middle of the 14th century that children in schools were again taught in English, and of course it was a different

A school: notice the birch stick

A scribe at work: look for inkwells, rush matting, a folding stool and paint pots

"English" from the language spoken before the Normans came to England, and had a lot of French words and meanings mixed up in it.

Boys who were probably going to be monks went to monastery schools and learnt to sing Latin hymns and songs, though they probably did not at first understand what the words meant. They also learnt their ABC and a little reading—of Latin sentences translated into French. Writing was not often taught, probably because Latin was the only language which had fixed rules of spelling. French and English were written just as they were pronounced, and as words were pronounced very differently in different areas, you can imagine how difficult it was to learn to read and write.

There were some fine new grammar schools established in the Middle Ages, to which boys were sent if they seemed likely to become good scholars. There they learnt mainly Latin grammar, which is why the schools were called "grammar" schools. "Grammar" meant more then than it does now—it meant how to write and speak correctly. The Bishop of Winchester in 1382 founded the first school which was not a part of a church or monastery. There were to be seventy "poor and needy" scholars, but these were boys from famous families and there was no idea of providing education for really poor people.

Chained books in a library

The boys had very long hours at school. Eton, founded in 1440, was a grammar school to which boys could go from all parts of England and not only from the immediate neighbourhood as was usual. For this reason it was called a "public" school. School at Eton began at 6 o'clock in the morning and went on until 9 o'clock, when there were prayers and a quarter of an hour for breakfast. Dinner was at 11. Afternoon school lasted from 1 until 5, except in summer when the boys rested until 3. On Sunday mornings the work was the same as on other days, but they had the afternoon off.

Most schools had only one master, and some of the cleverest boys helped to teach the others. There were prefects who had to report anyone found fighting, or with a dirty face or dirty clothes, or talking anything but Latin.

As well as grammar, these schools taught logic (how to argue and discuss well), and rhetoric (how to speak well in public). The boys often gathered in groups in the streets on a holiday and argued in Latin about some difficult problem.

The cleverest boys went on to learn arithmetic, geometry, music and astronomy. It may seem surprising to you that arithmetic was considered to be one of the difficult subjects, whereas quite young children start to learn it at school now. Medieval arithmetic was quite different from the arithmetic you do, because the numerals—the signs used for the numbers—were different.

Up to the 14th century Roman numerals were used throughout Europe, instead of the Arabic ones in use today. In the Roman method of counting I was 1, V was 5, X was 10, L was 50, C was 100, D, 500, and M, 1000. You made up your numbers by repeating the signs, so for 2 you wrote II, and for 3, III; but for 4 you wrote IV (1 less than 5) and for 6 you put VI (1 more than 5), so 7 was VII and 8 was VIII, but for 9 you put IX (1 less than 10). It is really quite simple when you understand it, but of course it was much more clumsy than the method we use today. For example, this sum $267 + 184 = 451$ would have been CCLXVII + CLXXXIV = CCCCLI, which you would have written CDLI. Indeed, Roman numerals were so clumsy that even clever mathematicians did their sums with an abacus. This was very like a bead-counting frame that small children play with nowadays.

The problems were very similar to those in modern sum-books. In the British Museum there is a manuscript of problems and questions, which was written in the 15th century. Here is one of the problems: "A swallow invited a snail to dinner; he lived just one league from the spot, and the snail travelled at the rate of an inch a day. How long would it be before he dined?"

Boys who were very clever went from a grammar school to one of the new centres of learning at Oxford or Cambridge, or Paris in France, or Bologna in Italy. These were called Universities. Boys went there at any time between thirteen and seventeen years old and studied such subjects as law, medicine or astronomy.

Poor children did not usually go to school at all, but learnt about life by helping their parents, neighbours and friends, as we have seen. There were some people who demanded that no villein's children should be allowed to go to school, because if they did it took so many workers off the land. But after 1406 a law was passed saying that every villein should have the right to send his sons and daughters to school if he wished. Many parents did not wish to, even if there was a school in their neighbourhood. They preferred to keep their children at home to help with the work.

Rich boys who did not go to school either had a tutor to teach them at home, or else they were sent away to be pages in the household of some grand friend or relation. Here they learned good manners and good behaviour. A boy had to know how to lay a table, carve a joint and serve it, and wait upon guests; how to dress and undress his lord, how to make a bed, serve wine, hold the silver basin in which his lord washed his hands at meal-times, and so on. Nobody thought there was anything undignified in waiting upon other people and young men and boys of very noble families were proud to serve others.

A bone stylus

A horn ink-well

A boy also learned how to dress himself neatly, to wash his face and hands, comb his hair, use a pocket-hand-kerchief, not to shuffle his feet, talk or drink with his mouth full, or play with his spoon and knife at meals—just as small children learn now at home. We can imagine how necessary it was to give instructions in such matters, for people had only a very small stock of clothes (unless they were very rich), and houses had no running water or lavatories.

Here are some of the instructions which were given to a boy when he started his training: "Do not claw your head or your back as if you were after a flea. Retch not, nor spit too far, nor laugh or speak too loud. Beware of making faces or scorning; and be no liar with your mouth. Do not lick your lips or drivel. . . . Do not lick a dish with your tongue to get out the dust. . . ."

We know very little about girls' education in the Middle Ages. They did not go to school. In poor families they helped at home and knew very little about book-learning; in wealthy ones they shared the tutor with their brother, or had a governess of their own, and learned to read and write. Often they were sent away from home as their brothers were, and went to be "waiting gentlewomen" in a nobleman's household. There they learnt to speak French, to curtsey gracefully, to do embroidery, to preserve fruit, to make perfumes and medicines and ointments, to play musical instruments, to dance and sing and spin.

As all books were written by hand, it is not surprising that none was written for the amusement of boys and girls. There were plenty of books of instruction, grammars, dictionaries, bestiaries (books of natural history, mainly about animals), but it did not occur to anyone, until several hundreds of years later, to write stories. But medieval children did hear a great many thrilling stories—some of them the same as the ones you hear and read—from the glee-men, who travelled about from village to village, staying in people's houses and entertaining them with stories and with ballads sung to the accompaniment of a harp.

The only books for children were horn books. They were not at all like our books nowadays. A horn book was really just a small page with the alphabet and one or two prayers written on it. Later, as we know, the page was printed.

The piece of paper was pasted on to a small oblong piece of wood and covered over with a thin sheet of horn through which the lettering could be clearly seen. The horn protected the paper from tearing, and from sticky fingers.

The piece of horn was bound round with a strip of brass and fixed with eight brass tacks with decorated heads. This "book" had a wooden handle, so that it looked rather like a small flat wooden bat. A string was threaded through a hole in the handle and you hung your "book" round your neck or from your girdle.

The alphabet had a little cross at the beginning and end, and sometimes children called their ABC their "Christ's cross row" and sometimes even "Criss cross row".

You would have been very unlikely to have a horn book of your own, except in a wealthy family. At school you had to share one with several other children. Probably you learnt your alphabet mainly by saying it out aloud all together. Much of the learning at school in the Middle Ages was done by heart and would seem dull to you nowadays. You were lucky if you had a good memory. Probably medieval boys and girls enjoyed some of what they learnt and found some of it dull. Here is a verse from a 15th-century poem, about a boy who played truant and was caught:

> I would my master were an hare,
> And all his bookes houndes were,
> And I myself a jolly hunter;
> To blow my horn I would not spare!
> For if he were dead I would not care.

No doubt some children *would* have cared, for, as we have seen, conditions varied a good deal. But on the whole teachers then ruled by fear and did not try to understand the children. They thought of them as little adults to be "licked into shape".

Horn books

Being burnt at the stake

The church was very much more important then than it is now and most of what people learnt came through their religion. When people thought about "the church", it was the Catholic Church whose headquarters was in Rome and whose head was the Bishop of Rome, called the Pope. All the churches and cathedrals of England were Roman Catholic. No man might think for himself about religion, or hold any views different from those decided by the Church. If he did, he was a heretic and could be burned at the stake. This did happen sometimes and it would have been a terrible and very exciting thing to go and see. The Church of England and other Protestant churches did not come into existence until much later.

Children went with their parents to Mass in the splendid new churches which were being built in many parts of the country and to little stone chapels which had been built in country places in the Norman style, with thick round pillars and rounded arches with zigzag carving over them. You would have learnt Latin hymns and prayers by heart and you learnt manners at church too, for there you had to curtsey and bow, and so on.

Whether you were rich or poor, townsman or countryman, grown-up, girl or boy, you went to Mass every day and you observed Sunday and Holy Days very strictly. You joined in religious processions as they passed through your village and you ran eagerly to the nearest cross-roads when you heard that a wandering friar was going to preach there on his way through the district.

You would have been used to seeing monks walking about your village, too, for there were a great many monasteries in England. There were also many nunneries, or convents, but the nuns did not go out a great deal.

Monks and nuns were people who gave up their possessions and decided that they would not marry and set up house as most people did, but would serve God in a very special way. They joined with other men or women and lived together and shared everything in common. They spent their time praying and looking after their monastery church; some of them started schools, others looked after old or ill people and travellers. Many were fine scholars and wrote learned books as well as books of prayer.

A friar preaching at the crossroads

A grey friar and black friar

Here is a complaint, written by a Bishop in the 14th century, about people who ill-treated books. The Bishop also blamed readers for eating fruit and cheese while looking at books, and using straw or flowers for book-markers!

". . . Especially, moreover, must we restrain impudent youths from handling books—these youths who, when they have learned to draw the shapes of letters, soon begin, if opportunity be granted them, to be uncouth scribblers on the best volumes and, where they see some larger margin above the text, make a show with monstrous letters . . . a practice which we have seen to be too often injurious to the best of books, both as concerns their usefulness and their price. . . . Let no crying child admire the pictures in the capital letters, lest he defile the parchment with his wet hand, for he touches instantly whatever he sees. Laymen, moreover, who look in the same way at a book lying upside down as when it is open in its natural way, are wholly unworthy the intercourse of books. . . . Again, a becoming cleanness of hands would add much to books and scholars. . . ."

Things to do and talk about

1 Make a list of some of the problems you might have heard your parents discussing at home in the Middle Ages.

2 Write in Roman numerals:
the number of people who live in your house
the number of children in your class
the date of your birthday
today's date.

3 Pretend that you are a scholar at Eton in the Middle Ages and write a letter to a boy or girl who was being taught at home by a tutor, telling them anything about your school which you think will be of interest.

4 Write a story about a family occasion nowadays and illustrate it with drawings in the margins, like the monks did.

5 Look at these lines from the early English printed version of the Canterbury Tales. Try to read some of it and then see how much you understand by reading the same lines in a modern version.

Whan that Aprill With his shouris sote
And the droughte of marche hath pad y rote
And badid every veyne in suche licour
Of Whiche vertu engendrid is the flour
Whanne zepherus eke With his sote breth
Enspirid hath in every holte and heth
The tendir croppis and the yong sonne
Hath in the ram half his cours y ronne
And smale foulis make melodie
That sleppy al nyght With oppy ye
So prikith hem nature in her corage
Than longyng folk to goy on pilgremage

73

9 Learning to be a knight

WHAT a medieval boy probably wanted more than anything else was to become a knight. If you were of a well-to-do family this was not so difficult, but it was almost impossible for a villein's son.

It was a great honour to be chosen by the king as especially brave, honest and gentle, and worthy to be knighted. You probably enjoyed listening to stories about King Arthur and his Knights of the Round Table and determined to do similar gallant deeds. But it took a very long time to learn all that was necessary.

As we have said in the chapter about education, a boy lived at home with his parents until he was about seven years old, and then he was sent away to become a page in the household of a nobleman who promised to train him to become a knight.

He spent much time serving his master and the ladies of the household, and learning to be polite and well-mannered. He learnt to serve at table, and to help his master to dress, for fashionable clothes were often very tight, and armour was heavy and difficult to put on. He was taught to wait upon the ladies and entertain them with songs which he accompanied on his lute. A knight was above all "chivalrous"—sporting in his behaviour and courteous, and considerate to ladies and to those weaker than himself. He also learnt to read, to ride well, to hunt and hawk, and to fight with a lance and a sword.

When he had been trained for about seven years, and if he had done well, he became a squire, that is, a young man who followed his master to battle. He had to keep his master's armour polished and shining for him, to be able to help him put it on and then mount his horse. He had to carry spare weapons and a spare helmet and he had to be ready to go to his master's help if he were wounded. In fact, by following his master in battle he learnt for himself

The ceremony of becoming a knight

how to behave bravely and unselfishly in time of danger.

Squires were in many ways like prefects in school. They had a lot of responsibilities, but they were still learning. They had fun among themselves and used to have tournaments of their own and play many games which helped them to learn to be brave and very quick in seeing danger and in facing it.

When his master considered that his squire was ready to become a knight, he arranged a very solemn ceremony, usually at some great feast such as Christmas or Easter time. The night before, the squire "kept vigil" in the church—that is, he knelt all night before the altar and prayed that he might prove worthy to be a true knight. In the morning there was a solemn mass, or service, to which his friends and family came. When the mass was ended the squire had to kneel down and take an oath to be true and faithful. Then an important noble, or sometimes even the king himself, girded the squire's belt and sword on him, and kissed him on the cheek as a sign of peace. Attendants fastened on his spurs and so the squire became a knight.

Hawking

There was great rejoicing at such times and in the evening there was usually a great feast held and everyone was very proud of the new knight.

War was almost an everyday thing in the Middle Ages, although it was often only local. There were always quarrels of one kind or another going on between rival barons or between the king and some of his nobles, and so to be a knight and to fight for a cause meant that you always had plenty to do. In return for service to the king or to an important lord, you might be given land and money.

A tournament

Girls, of course, could not train to become knights, but they, as well as the boys, must often have been thrilled to see a band of knights riding through the village. Their armour covered them entirely and their helm covered most of their faces, so they wore brightly-coloured labels of various kinds so that they could be recognised and could recognise one another in battle. These labels did not have their names written on them, but the "device" of their family or of their lord's family.

The broad, smooth surface of the shield was one place where a picture-label was useful. And when a linen garment, called a surcoat, began to be worn over the metal armour, it usually had a device embroidered or "emblazoned" on it in bright colours.

Knights in chain mail with heraldic devices on their shields, banners and surcoats

A knight before going into battle

The trappings of the horses also had devices embroidered on them, and every knight was allowed to carry a pennon, or small flag with a forked tail. If he distinguished himself in battle he was then allowed to carry a square banner instead of a pennon. Sometimes a crest was worn on the helmet, too, and these were sometimes very large.

The study of these medieval badges is called heraldry. Here are various heraldic signs, or devices, but you will have to imagine them in bright, bold colours.

To give young knights practice and to entertain everybody, tournaments and jousts were held. These were mock fights between two groups of knights, or between two knights only. The audience wore their best clothes and gathered round to watch. The aim was not to kill your opponent, but to break his lance and unhorse him. They used lances with blunt points, and umpires kept a score in points and disqualified any knight who inflicted a foul blow. At the end of the day the winner was presented with a prize by a lady who had been declared the queen of the tournament.

Gradually, as gunpowder began to be used for fighting battles, it became less necessary for knights to be able to use their lances and shields skilfully and so tournaments gradually died out. Probably the boys and girls were very sorry when this happened, for it was certainly the most exciting day of the year, when you managed to squeeze into the enclosure and watch some splendid knights fighting.

A tournament between two knights

Things to do and talk about

(left) *Reproduction of a rubbing of the Braunche Brass in St. Margaret's Church, King's Lynn.*

1 Practise cutting a thick piece of polystyrene and then carve a knight from it. You can dress the figure from scraps of leather, milk bottle tops and pieces of foil, pinned on.

2 You can make an attractive frieze of knights fighting at a tournament if you draw the outline of each figure and fill it in with small pieces of screwed-up tissue paper stuck on.

3 Find a church with a memorial brass of a knight. Get permission to make a rubbing and mount and label it carefully. The illustration is of a rubbing of the Braunche Brass in St. Margaret's Church, King's Lynn.

4 Visit a castle if you can and write a story about an exciting day when a tournament was held there, or when the king paid a visit.

5 You will probably have guessed which of the pictures of Chaucer's Pilgrims is the **knight**. He had travelled in Europe fighting for the Christian faith against the Turks. Find out all you can about the Crusades.

10 Playing

ALTHOUGH everyone in the Middle Ages lived much less comfortably than we do nowadays, life was more exciting for most people and both children and grown-ups found a great deal of fun in simple things. There were none of the mechanical ways of amusing yourself that we can enjoy now: no cinema, no radio, no record-player, no television; there were no books to read, no concerts to go to, very few visitors and no excursions to the seaside. Almost everyone lived in the country and all the people of a village would gather together and make up their own games and amusements. Everyday life was in some ways very like camping— people did things for themselves far more than we do and of course boys and girls always like that.

Music was much enjoyed, but people then did not just listen to music; they made it themselves. Most people could play some kind of instrument and enjoyed singing to themselves and to each other. Tunes were not written down. Somebody started a tune out of their head; someone else repeated it, perhaps with an addition or an alteration, until in the end the prettiest, or liveliest or easiest tune would be the one which everyone joined in with and knew by heart. All the popular tunes were simple, with no large jumps between the notes, because these would have been harder to remember. There were jolly tunes for hunting, sad ones for partings, rousing ones for battles, and catchy tunes which people sang to help them on with monotonous jobs in the fields or about the house.

Look for bagpipes, drums, cymbals, bells,
horns, stringed instruments, hand organs and
zithers, and the dog carrying a collecting bowl

Many of the tunes were about out-of-door things and the very first one to be written down was called "Summer is i-cumen (coming) in". Part of the manuscript is illustrated opposite.

Many of our folk-songs and country-dances come from tunes which were popular in the Middle Ages and people used often to dance while they sang. Minstrels went from manor to manor and they carried news and gossip with them and often sang it, instead of saying it. They also sang ballads, which are songs with stories in them, and of course the boys and girls learnt the tunes and put their own words to them if they did not understand the grown-up ones. Sometimes the wandering minstrels went about in pairs—one would sing and play an instrument, while the other would dance, or do juggling tricks to the music.

Girls enjoyed dressing-up in the Middle Ages as much as they do now, but the clothes which the grown-ups passed on to their children then seem, to our eyes, to be much more attractive for dressing up than any clothes which our mothers and fathers pass on nowadays.

Boys playing bob-apple

From the song "Sumer is i-cumen in, loud sing cuckoo", written about 1225

Hunting on horseback. One rider is sounding
the horn

Hunting was a very popular pastime for grown-ups
and sometimes children were allowed to join in too.
Anyway it would have been fun to run alongside the horses
and hounds at the beginning of a hunt and to play about
and wait for them to return with their booty. Young
children had hobby-horses and rocking-horses to pretend
with, and toy animals of all sorts cut out of wood to play
hunting with.

People loved hawking as much as they did hunting.
Hawks are wild birds that can be tamed and taught to catch
other birds. So hawking was a kind of hunting, with a bird
instead of hounds. You carried the hawk on your left hand,
and you had to wear gloves because the bird's claws were
sharp. The hawk had leather straps fastened round its
legs so that it could be held easily, and a cloth or a hood
covering its eyes when it was not in flight. Sometimes
hawks had little silver bells on their legs, so that they tinkled
when they were flying. The bird was released when there
were other birds for it to chase and catch and it brought
them back to its master. Hawks have very sharp eyes and we
sometimes still say that so-and-so has "eyes like a hawk"
if his eyesight is very keen.

Hunting on foot with bow and arrow

Children's games: tilting at the quintain on a wooden horse, a swinging quintain, playing at tournament on foot and pick-a-back, whip tops, skittles and whirling stick

Water quintain

All boys learnt to shoot with bow and arrows, just like their fathers, and spent a great deal of time practising. They learnt to fight like their fathers too, but with blunt lances and small shields, and often played at "tilting" their lances against a target. There was a favourite fighting game which used to be played in boats at Easter-time by those who lived near a river. A pole was stuck up in mid-stream and a shield hung on it. The idea was to see who could hit the middle of the shield with his lance, while standing in a boat which floated quickly down-stream. It was a very easy matter to over-balance, and there were boats nearby ready to rescue anyone who fell into the water. A writer describing the game in the 12th century tells us: "Upon the bridge, wharfes and houses by the riverside stand great numbers, to see and laugh thereat".

The same writer tells us that "in the holy days (holidays) all the summer the youths are exercised in leaping, dancing, shooting, wrestling, casting the stone, and practising their shields; the maidens trip to their timbrels and dance as long as they can well see".

Boys playing trapball

There were no games organised at school as there are nowadays, but there were plenty of ball games of one kind or another which boys, and girls too, played. Some were more or less like hockey, others like tennis or rounders. Girls played stoolball, which was rather like our cricket. In some districts boys and girls still play stoolball today.

Most of these ball games were played in the streets and sometimes they caused serious disturbance to passersby. Football was a particularly wild game, not played at all as we play it nowadays, with a fixed number of players on each side and with definite rules and regular goals. It was a wild struggle between opposite sides, to force the ball through the streets from one end of the town or village to another. There were no rules at all and players often had their legs broken. On one or two occasions a football player was killed in the scramble. Bowls and quoits were also played in the streets.

Winters seem often to have been much colder than they are now and rivers, marshes and flooded fields were often covered with thick ice for months at a time. Snowballing, tobogganing and skating were very popular, especially with boys and girls. They wore rough skates made of the leg-bones of animals.

You would have enjoyed keeping pet animals in the Middle Ages, as perhaps you do now. As well as tame hawks and hounds and horses, medieval families had pet birds like thrushes, robins, falcons, which are like hawks but bigger, and dogs and cats to look after and play with.

But medieval people often used animals in ways which seem to us to be very cruel. Two popular pastimes were bull-baiting and bear-baiting. People used to gather round to see a bull or a bear worried to death by dogs which were set upon it. Cock-fighting was also popular: special cocks were trained so that they were very quarrelsome and fought when they were set upon one another. Schoolboys used to amuse themselves sometimes by throwing sticks at a cock which was tied by a leg to a post. Such things were quite normal and people did not realise that they were cruel. Nowadays, of course, we are shocked by anyone who hurts or teases a defenceless animal, and if people do so they can be punished.

On special feast days and holy days there were great festivities, which the children from miles around came to see. There were processions to watch, minstrels singing the latest songs, jugglers and tumblers doing wonderful tricks and dancing and turning somersaults to amuse the crowd.

Bear baiting

85

Some of the people you might have seen on the way to the fair

On certain days the members of the guilds performed plays and if you were an apprentice you would probably have acted a part in one of them. The plays were not performed in a theatre, but on high carts which were drawn through the streets while the acting went on, so that everyone could see and listen when the cart went by. The plays told familiar stories from the Bible and from old legends, so people knew what was happening and could enjoy and understand the story without seeing the whole of the play.

From the 12th century onwards plays were acted just outside the city of London, at Clerkenwell not far from the modern Sadlers Wells Theatre. If you lived in London you would probably have enjoyed going to see these plays, and you might even have been one of the people the Prioress of Clerkenwell complained to the King about. Here is a petition she made in the early 14th century:

"To our Lord the King. The poor Prioress of Clerkenwell prays that he will to provide and order a remedy because the people of London lay waste and destroy her corn and grass by their miracle plays and wrestling matches so that she has no profit of them, nor can have any unless the king have pity for they are a savage folk and we cannot stand against them and cannot get justice by any law. So, Sire, for God's sake have pity upon us".

Medieval children did not have nearly as many toys as most modern boys and girls do. Babies were no doubt given something soft to cuddle, just as they are now. Girls had dolls, usually made of wood, but dolls' houses were not known. And there were no prams for babies, so certainly there were none for dolls. Boys played with little wooden carts, wooden skittles, skipping-ropes, balls, tops, and kites. There were no mechanical toys, needless to say.

Grown-ups played many games that now belong to children only. "Hoodman Blind" was one of these that the whole family would play together. It was very like Blind-man's-buff, except that the player in the middle was blinded by having his hood fixed over his head, instead of a handkerchief tied round it. The other players took off their hoods and tried to hit him with them without being caught themselves. Sometimes the ends of the hoods were knotted and it must have hurt when you were hit with them. Another game of the same kind was "Hot Cockles", but in this the player in the middle had to kneel down blind-folded and try to catch one of the others before they knocked him down. Nearly all the games were much rougher in the Middle Ages than those we play nowadays, and there were very few rules.

Children watching puppets

Playing draughts

Things to do and talk about

1 Work with a group of your friends to make a wall-chart of medieval children playing. It will look better if you put buildings in the background.

2 Discuss whether the medieval pastimes of bull-baiting, bear-baiting and cock-fighting were more cruel, or less, than fox-hunting, pheasant-shooting or fishing are nowadays.

3 How many musical instruments can you identify in this illustration of a church carving?

4 Find out more about these sports and entertainments in the Middle Ages.

The Bull Ring	Golf
Chess	Football
Mummers	**Bear Baiting**
Skating	Jesters
Hockey	

11 Travelling about

Most boys and girls nowadays are used to travelling about a great deal. Perhaps you, for instance, have to go quite a long distance to and from school or to visit friends and relatives, or you may go out into the country on your bicycle or by coach or train for day trips; and most families go away from home for a holiday once a year, or even more. And it is not very unusual for the father of a family to change his job so that the whole family has to move and settle down somewhere else.

In the Middle Ages, however, people did not usually change their jobs. They stayed in the same place, doing the same kind of work, for most of their lives. They did not go away for holidays either, and their friends mostly lived nearby. Nevertheless, some people travelled about a good deal, as we shall see later.

A dog cart and a donkey cart

A royal journey. The ladies are riding in a
leather-covered wagon

The roads were in a very bad state, for most of them
were either rough cart tracks across the country, or were
the roads which the Romans had built centuries before,
but which had not been properly repaired since. They were
full of pot-holes and deep cart-ruts; in winter you very
easily got stuck in deep mud and in summer the surface
was dry and dusty. No wonder most people either walked
or went on horseback, instead of bumping along in a rough
kind of cart, which might often overturn.

There was also great danger that, if you travelled about,
you might be attacked by wild beasts or by dangerous men.
In many places the thick woods at the side of the road were
cut down in order that wolves, bears, wild bulls, wild boars
or stags could not take shelter there. Even worse, there
were many thieves, brigands, outlaws and highwaymen
who lay in wait for unarmed travellers.

So travelling was difficult and dangerous, yet there were
always a number of people going from place to place and if
you sat down by the side of the road near your home you
might see all sorts of interesting and exciting sights.

The King always journeyed about a great deal and you might see a large procession of nobles, soldiers and members of the Royal household, passing by on horseback or in litters drawn by horses. The Court did not stay in one place for long but travelled from one castle or manor to another. When roads were so bad it was easier to take men and horses to their food than to bring the food to them. It is recorded that King Edward I, in the 13th century, changed his house 75 times during one single year!

The King's important officials did the same as he did, and so the chief roads in England were often crowded with people moving from place to place. You might see a couple of judges going on horseback from the court of one town to that of another, with their clerks riding behind them carrying rolls of parchment. You might see a group of monks travelling from one monastery to discuss matters with those of another, or bands of merchants going to one of the great fairs.

Travellers on horseback

If it was summer time you might well see a band of pilgrims passing through. Pilgrims were men and women —and sometimes boys and girls went with them—who left their homes to go and visit places where good men had lived or worked or had been buried. Often they went on long and dangerous journeys so that they could say their prayers or offer a present in a particular church or at the tomb or shrine of a saint.

In England the chief places to which pilgrims went were the tomb of King Edward the Confessor in Westminster Abbey, that of St. Alban in the town of St. Albans, and that of St. Cuthbert in the great cathedral at Durham, in Northumberland. The shrine of St. Edmund at Bury St. Edmund's was also a favourite place for pilgrims to go to, and the holy tree at Glastonbury. People from all parts of England, and those from other countries too, liked to go to Canterbury, to the tomb of St. Thomas à Becket, the Archbishop who had been murdered there by the King's orders in the 12th century. You can still see the stone steps in Canterbury Cathedral, worn by the knees of the pilgrims who went to the shrine to pray, and in Chaucer's *Canterbury Tales* you can read the kind of stories that pilgrims told one another to pass away the time on the way.

Sometimes English people went on long pilgrimages to other countries too, and you might even see a band setting off to the Holy Land, to visit the places where Jesus had lived. They would have a long and very dangerous journey to Palestine, and many people who began it did not come back again. Before they started on the long journey home they bought a badge at the shrine they had visited, to show their friends that they had really been on a pilgrimage. Some people seem to have spent most of their time travelling about from one shrine to another, collecting badges as they went. Perhaps they wore them all at once, as some boys and girls wear other sorts of badges nowadays!

You might possibly see a large army of people setting out for the Holy Land, though not to go on pilgrimage. They were Crusaders, going to help pilgrims who had been badly treated, or even put to death, by the Turks who were not Christians. The Turks, who were brave and gallant fighters, were followers of the Prophet Mohammed, and believed that Christians should be treated as slaves. You knew which people were going to fight in the Holy Land, for they wore a cross on their cloak. The Latin word for "cross' is "crux", and that is why those wars were called "Crusades". It was exciting, but sad, to see them setting off, for only very few expected to come home again.

A tinker and a beggar woman

A pilgrim. Notice his staff and the cockleshell badges on his hat and purse. He carried a leather water bottle and a small metal one for holy water

There were some people you might have seen passing, who were not travelling to any particular place, but who spent all their lives wandering from village to village, just as tramps do nowadays. You might see a pedlar, with a pack on his back laden with ribbons, furs, laces, buttons and other goods which people were pleased to buy.

Then there might be soldiers passing through, going off to fight against some noble who was threatening an attack, beggars trying to scrounge a living, or criminals fleeing from justice. It would have been a specially exciting day if a "hue and cry" had been raised in the district to chase such a man, and everyone nearby dropped whatever they were doing and tried to catch him before he got away.

One of the chief difficulties of travellers was to cross rivers and streams. In some places there were bridges which had been built by rich men as a gift to their town or village, or paid for by money which the local people had joined together to collect. It was nobody's particular business to attend to such things as the upkeep of roads or bridges. Sometimes bridges were in such bad repair that they broke or were swept away when the river was in flood.

There were many fords across rivers. A ford is a crossing shallow enough for horses and men to wade across. Sometimes a town grew up at a ford, and such towns often still have names ending in "ford"—like Bradford or Hereford or Hertford.

The travellers did not all have somewhere to sleep at night. The king and other important people usually stayed at a monastery. Merchants and others who could afford it stayed at an inn, but poorer people had to camp out in the open, in spite of danger and discomfort, unless they were lucky enough to find some kind person who would give them a meal and a night's lodging. Many people were pleased to do so, because that was almost the only way there was of hearing the news of the world outside your own district. Probably the boys and girls all wanted to stay up and listen, even though it was long past their bedtime. They must have heard wonderful tales of adventure danger, excitement and fun.

Things to do and talk about

1 Make a frieze of travellers you might have seen near your home in the Middle Ages. You could cut the figures out of thick paper and dress them with scraps of fabric stuck on; the rich people could have buttons, sequins, feathers and pieces of foil for decoration. The pictures of the Canterbury Pilgrims you will have seen on these pages will help you.

2 Make a picture map of England for your classroom wall, showing the route the pilgrims took from London to Canterbury and the towns and villages which were there in Chaucer's day. Mark in other medieval shrines too.

3 Make a list of as many towns as you can which end in -ford. What does this tell us about them?

4 Discuss the dangers and difficulties of travelling in the Middle Ages and compare them with those we have to put up with nowadays.

5 Study this picture of a toll-keeper receiving payment for crossing a bridge. Are there any toll bridges left?

2291